Cheetah

Rusty-spotted cat

Tigers fighting

What is a big cat?

The five main big cats are the mightiest members of the cat family. These fierce, furry animals have striking fur, super senses, and powerful bodies suited to high-speed hunting in the wild. They are among the world's best-known mammals and some of the most successful in hunting animals to eat.

Snow leopard

Jaguar

Tail

A long, thick tail helps big cats keep their balance while chasing animals to eat, called prey. The tail also helps cats change direction or climb trees.

Tiger

Claws

A cat's sharp claws are retractable. This means they can be withdrawn or extended as necessary.

DK | Penguin Random House

Project editor Clare Lloyd
Project art editor Emma Hobson
Senior editor Marie Greenwood
Assistant editors Shalini Agrawal, Shambhavi Thatte
US senior editor Shannon Beatty
US editor Elizabeth Searcy
Art editor Shipra Jain
Senior art editor Nidhi Mehra
DTP designers Anita Yadav, Mohammad Rizwan
Picture researcher Sakshi Saluja
Jacket co-ordinator Francesca Young
Jacket designer Kartik Gera
Educational consultant Jacqueline Harris
Managing editors Laura Gilbert, Alka Thakur Hazarika
Managing art editors Diane Peyton Jones,
Romi Chakraborty
Delhi team head Malavika Talukder
Senior pre-production producer Tony Phipps
Senior producer Isabell Schart
Creative director Helen Senior
Publishing director Sarah Larter

First American Edition 2019
Published in the United States by DK Publishing
345 Hudson Street, New York, New York 10014

Copyright © 2019 Dorling Kindersley Limited
DK, a Division of Penguin Random House LLC
19 20 21 22 23 10 9 8 7 6 5 4 3 2 1
001–311567–Feb/2019

A catalog record for this book is available from the
Library of Congress.
ISBN 978-1-4654-7929-7 (Flexibound)
ISBN 978-1-4654-7930-3 (Hardcover)

DK books are available at special discounts when purchased in bulk
for sales promotions, premiums, fund-raising, or educational use.
For details, contact: DK Publishing Special Markets, 345 Hudson
Street, New York, New York 10014 SpecialSales@dk.com

Printed and bound in China

A WORLD OF IDEAS:
SEE ALL THERE IS TO KNOW

www.dk.com

Contents

Ocelot

Snow leopard

Caracal

DKfindout!
Big Cats

Author: Andrea Mills
Consultant: Giles Clark

Things to find out:

The origins of the cat family can be traced back more than 25 million years. Ancient ancestors evolved (developed) into eight lineages, or family lines, of cats, with all of them shown here.

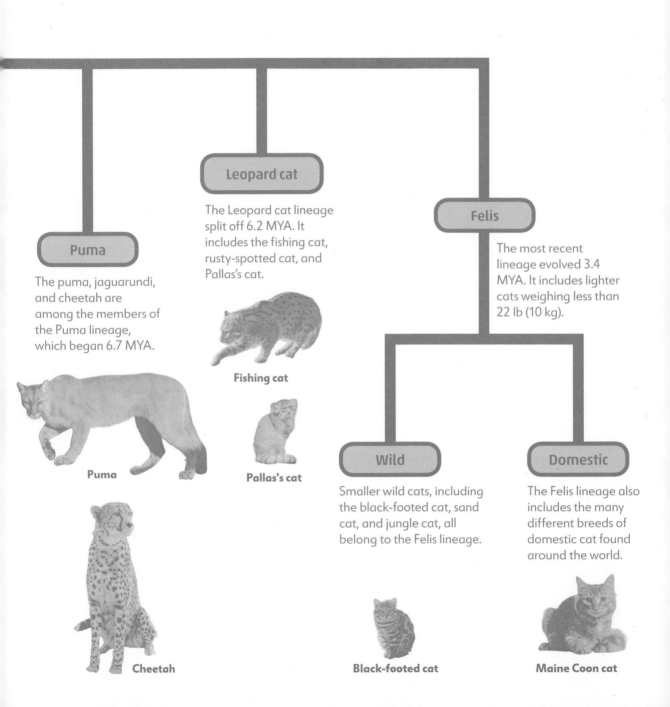

Puma

The puma, jaguarundi, and cheetah are among the members of the Puma lineage, which began 6.7 MYA.

Puma

Cheetah

Leopard cat

The Leopard cat lineage split off 6.2 MYA. It includes the fishing cat, rusty-spotted cat, and Pallas's cat.

Fishing cat

Pallas's cat

Felis

The most recent lineage evolved 3.4 MYA. It includes lighter cats weighing less than 22 lb (10 kg).

Wild

Smaller wild cats, including the black-footed cat, sand cat, and jungle cat, all belong to the Felis lineage.

Black-footed cat

Domestic

The Felis lineage also includes the many different breeds of domestic cat found around the world.

Maine Coon cat

Fur

Patterned coats are the perfect camouflage for big cats. They help them blend in with their surroundings and hide from prey.

Lion

Teeth

Big cats have large, pointed canine teeth and back teeth like scissors. They use these teeth to cut into meat and break it into small chunks that are easy to swallow.

Leopard

Legs

With long and powerful legs, big cats can chase down their prey at breathtaking speeds.

Balancing act
Pet cats use their tails to balance on the branches of trees, narrow ledges, or fences.

Feline fur
Most pet cats have fur with patterns similar to those of big cats.

Domestic cats

Pet cats are generally smaller than big cats. They are tame, or domesticated, animals who are used to being near people. Many pet cats enjoy the safety of a secure home and regular meals and love to cuddle up to their owners. However, if pet cats are neglected, they soon turn wild (feral) and learn to look after themselves—just like big cats!

Pet cat or big cat?

Whether a pet cat or a big cat, all cats (or felines) have similar features. These include big eyes, long whiskers, sharp teeth, and claws that scratch. However, while big cats need to hunt for survival, most domestic cats are used to being fed and cared for by humans.

Playful paws
Retractable claws are most often extended to scratch posts, but they can also be used to catch mice and birds.

Cat camouflage
A big cat's patterned coat helps it hide in thick undergrowth and grassland.

Big cats

While a domestic cat may bring home a mouse as a present for its owner, big cats, such as this jaguar, must feed regularly in order to live. Their bodies are built for high-speed chasing and expert hunting. Except for the sociable lion, most big cats live alone.

Hunter hearing
The ears of big cats are sensitive to even the slightest sound carried over a long distance.

! WOW!

The **ancient Egyptians** first domesticated wild cats for **hunting rats and mice.**

FACT FILE

» **Weight:** 37–680 lb (17–310 kg)

» **Life expectancy:** up to 20 years

» **Speed:** up to 74 mph (120 kph)

» **Sleep:** up to 20 hours

» **Habitat:** forests, mountains, jungles, grasslands, and deserts

» **Diet:** raw meat

Killer claws
Almost all big cats have very sharp, retractable claws to take down and tear into prey.

Meet the big cats

Here are the five main big cats. Except for the snow leopard, which cannot, they are the only cats that can roar. They are among the top hunters, or predators, in the habitats they call home. While big cats prey on smaller and weaker animals in order to stay alive, no animal hunts big cats for food.

» Scale

Tiger

The biggest and heaviest cat is the tiger. This solitary hunter stalks its prey under cover of darkness. Tigers live in Asia, ranging from India's steamy tropics to Siberia's icy forests.

FACT FILE

» **Length:** 6 ft 6 in–11 ft 6 in (2–3.5 m)

» **Weight:** up to 700 lb (318 kg)

» **Continent:** Asia

» **Habitat:** tropical rainforests and conifer forests

Tigers use their long back legs to leap up to 23 ft (7 m).

» Scale

Lion

Nicknamed the "king of the jungle," the lion is known for its majestic mane and thunderous roar. Unlike most big cats, lions live in family groups, called prides. Here, hunting is a team effort.

FACT FILE

» **Length:** 4 ft 7 in–8 ft 2 in (1.4–2.5 m)

» **Weight:** up to 420 lb (250 kg)

» **Continent:** Africa and India

» **Habitat:** grasslands

Leopard

This big cat is an expert climber, spending much of its time high in the trees. Leopards live alone, hunt at night, and can carry their prey up into leafy branches to deter scavengers.

» Scale

Jaguar

The largest cat in the Americas is the jaguar. Found in wetter regions, this cat is a strong swimmer and targets prey in rivers as well as on land.

FACT FILE

» **Length:** 3 ft 3 in–6 ft 6 in (1–2 m)

» **Weight:** up to 220 lb (100 kg)

» **Continent:** Central and South America

» **Habitat:** forests and marshlands

» Scale

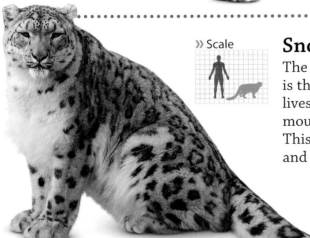

» Scale

Snow leopard

The most secretive big cat is the snow leopard, which lives high in the snowcapped mountains of central Asia. This feline has woolly fur and uses its tail for balance.

FACT FILE

» **Length:** 3 ft 7 in (1.1 m)

» **Weight:** up to 120 lb (55 kg)

» **Continent:** Asia

» **Habitat:** mountains

A snow leopard's furry tail doubles as a blanket.

Wild cats

Although not as large, wild cats share many of the same physical characteristics as the five big cats. Camouflaged coats help conceal them from the prey they hunt. However, unlike most of the big cats, none of these wild cats can roar.

! WOW!

Talented tree climbers, clouded leopards can **hang upside down** by their back legs!

Clouded leopard

Called the "tree tiger" in Malaysia, the clouded leopard is a tree-climbing forest dweller in Southeast Asia. It is the same size as a small leopard but has a coat whose pattern resembles dusky clouds. This solitary cat hunts deer, monkeys, and pigs.

» Scale

FACT FILE

» **Length:** 2 ft 11 in (0.9 m)

» **Weight:** up to 50 lb (23 kg)

» **Continent:** Asia

» **Habitat:** forests

Cheetah

The fastest animal on land is the cheetah. A long and flexible backbone propels the cheetah to record-breaking speeds across the African grasslands, or savannah.

FACT FILE

» **Length:** 3 ft 3 in–5 ft (1–1.5 m)

» **Weight:** up to 155 lb (70 kg)

» **Continent:** Africa

» **Habitat:** grasslands

» Scale

Puma

The first European settlers in the Americas mistook the puma for a lion. The puma can jump the farthest of all cats, covering 40 ft (20 m) in a single leap.

» Scale

FACT FILE

» **Length:** 8 ft 2 in (2.5 m)

» **Weight:** up to 220 lb (100 kg)

» **Continent:** North and South America

» **Habitat:** forests and mountains

» Scale

FACT FILE

» **Length:** 4 ft 3 in (1.3 m)

» **Weight:** up to 66 lb (30 kg)

» **Continent:** Europe and Asia

» **Habitat:** forests and scrublands

Eurasian lynx

One of Europe's largest predators, the Eurasian lynx has the power to hunt deer. It also eats smaller prey, including foxes and rabbits.

Smaller wild cats

Wild cats can be quite small—some are even smaller than domestic pets. Despite their small size, the patterned fur, lightweight bodies, and soundless movements of these cats make them successful hunters in their habitats, or homes.

» Scale

Ocelot

This American wild cat is about twice the size of a pet cat. It sleeps in foliage (leafy plants) during the day and hunts mice and other rodents when it gets dark.

FACT FILE

» **Length:** 3 ft 3 in (1 m)

» **Weight:** up to 44 lb (20 kg)

» **Continent:** North and South America

» **Habitat:** forests and grasslands

» Scale

Serval

Long legs and a tall neck allow the spotted serval to see over high savannah grass. The speedy serval also has large ears and an excellent sense of hearing.

» Scale

FACT FILE

» **Length:** 2 ft 6 in (0.7 m)

» **Weight:** up to 40 lb (18 kg)

» **Continent:** Africa and Asia

» **Habitat:** forests, grasslands, and deserts

Caracal

This small wild cat has long legs and is a great leaper. It is one of few cats with large, black-tipped tufted ears.

FACT FILE

» **Length:** 2 ft 7 in (0.8 m)

» **Weight:** up to 40 lb (18 kg)

» **Continent:** Africa

» **Habitat:** grasslands

Bobcat

The most common cat in North America is the bobcat. Unlike other wild cats, this solitary hunter has a very short tail.

» Scale

FACT FILE

» **Length:** 2 ft 4 in (0.7 m)

» **Weight:** up to 40 lb (18 kg)

» **Continent:** North America

» **Habitat:** forests, swamps, and deserts

Rusty-spotted cat

The world's smallest wild cat, the rusty-spotted cat comes from Asia. Smaller than most domestic cats, it weighs about 200 times less than a lion.

» Scale

» Scale

FACT FILE

» **Length:** 1 ft 4 in (0.4 m)

» **Weight:** up to 3 lb (1.4 kg)

» **Continent:** Asia

» **Habitat:** forests and grasslands

Sand cat

This desert dweller escapes the heat by sleeping in a sand burrow during the day and hunts lizards and mice at night.

FACT FILE

» **Length:** 1 ft 8 in (0.5 m)

» **Weight:** up to 6 lb 8 oz (3 kg)

» **Continent:** Africa and Asia

» **Habitat:** deserts

Fishing cat

This strong swimmer lives in wet regions of Asia. Fishing cats dive into water to catch fish, either in their mouths or between their webbed paws.

» Scale

FACT FILE

» **Length:** 2 ft 7 in (0.8 m)

» **Weight:** up to 20 lb (9 kg)

» **Continent:** Asia

» **Habitat:** forests and wetlands

Spots

A spotted coat provides perfect camouflage in sunny grasslands. The light base color with darker spots helps cats go unnoticed in the long grass. This gives a big cat cover while lying in wait for prey.

Stripes

Tigers are known for their striking striped fur, but they also have striped skin underneath. Most tigers are orange and black to help keep them camouflaged in the rainforest, where there are lots of plants, trees, and shrubs.

A tiger's stripes help keep them hidden when they are stalking prey.

Black tear marks run from the inside corners of a cheetah's eyes to the outside corners of its mouth.

Fur and markings

Cats are known for their stunning coats. Fur protects the skin and keeps cats warm. Colored markings break up their outline, which helps cats blend in with their surroundings, making them harder to spot. This is called camouflage. Colors and markings vary according to the habitat where each cat lives and hunts.

Rosettes

This rose-like pattern can completely cover the fur, appear in clumps, or have spots in the center. Dark rosettes on cream fur break up the cat's outline, making the cat hard to see in the dappled light of its habitat.

Black fur

Some cats are almost entirely covered in thick, black fur. However, if you look closely, you can see this black jaguar's markings are still there. Many cats hunt at night and creep up on prey behind a cloak of darkness.

This beautiful coat acts as camouflage when the leopard is on the move.

Unsuspecting prey stand little chance when a black jaguar prepares to pounce.

WOW!

No **two tigers** look the same. **Every tiger** has its own **unique stripe pattern,** like your **fingerprints!**

Clean coats

Big cats are often seen using their rough tongues to lick themselves. This keeps the fur clean and spreads natural oil, helping keep the coat smooth. Licking the fur also keeps cats cool in the hot tropical regions where many species live.

Tiger grooming

Inside a big cat

Beneath the furry coat of a big cat lies a bony skeleton. The skeletons of big cats are very similar to one another. They share a flexible backbone, strong legs, and wide jaws. The arrangement of the bones is perfect for speedy running and skilled hunting.

Sturdy skeleton

The big cat body is held together by a framework of about 250 bones. This protects the vital organs and gives cats fast and fluid movement in the limbs. The skeleton shown here is a tiger's.

Tail
Used for balance, the huge tail measures about 3 ft (1 m) in length.

Legs
The back legs are much longer than the front legs, which makes leaping and climbing easier.

Feline features

Big cats have skeletal and muscular systems that are suited to their lifestyle. Sharp teeth and powerful muscles are essential for successful hunting.

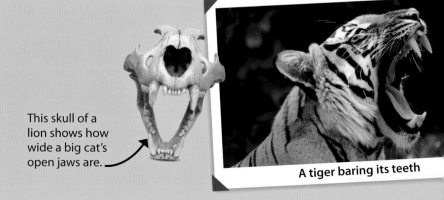

This skull of a lion shows how wide a big cat's open jaws are.

A tiger baring its teeth

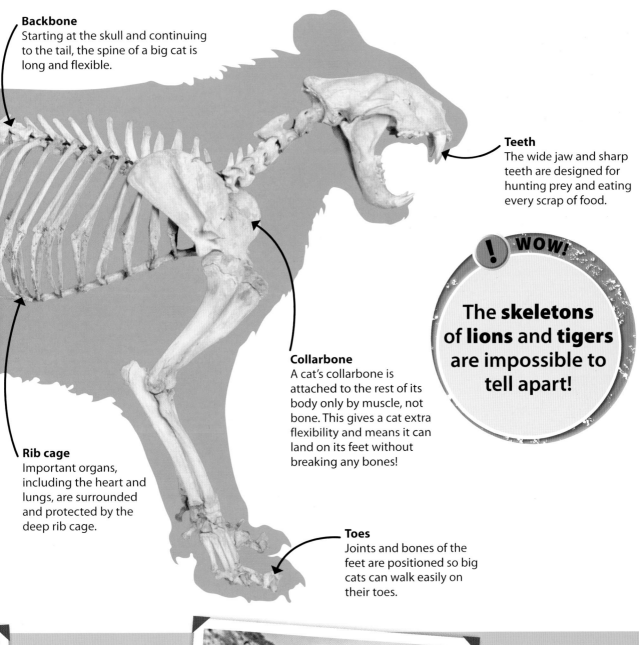

Backbone
Starting at the skull and continuing to the tail, the spine of a big cat is long and flexible.

Teeth
The wide jaw and sharp teeth are designed for hunting prey and eating every scrap of food.

! WOW!

The **skeletons** of **lions** and **tigers** are impossible to tell apart!

Collarbone
A cat's collarbone is attached to the rest of its body only by muscle, not bone. This gives a cat extra flexibility and means it can land on its feet without breaking any bones!

Rib cage
Important organs, including the heart and lungs, are surrounded and protected by the deep rib cage.

Toes
Joints and bones of the feet are positioned so big cats can walk easily on their toes.

Strong jaws
Cats have strong jaws and teeth. When a cat eats, the jaws open wide to help the cat break the tough bones of its prey.

A puma leaping off rocky mountains

Mighty muscles
Strong muscles in their long back legs help big cats jump long distances and pounce on prey from high up.

Superior senses

Big cats have heightened senses, which are far better developed than ours. A big cat's senses need to work well together when it's hunting alone at night. Eyes closely observe surroundings; the ears detect even the slightest sound; and the nose can sniff out any creature close by.

Sight

The eyesight of a big cat is six times better than that of a human. They have big, bright eyes with pupils that change size depending on light levels. At night, the pupils expand to let light flood in, giving cats excellent night vision.

The pupils get much smaller in bright sunlight.

TASTE

A long, rough tongue ensures big cats can taste different prey, recognize rotten meat, and get pieces of meat off the bone. Their tongues have no sweet receptors, so they are not interested in eating anything sweet!

Jacobson's organ

A special organ in the roof of the mouth allows big cats to accurately identify different scents from other cats and analyze them. They use this information to communicate with each other.

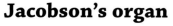
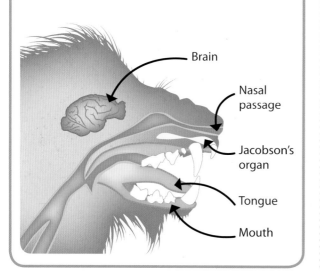

Brain

Nasal passage

Jacobson's organ

Tongue

Mouth

Smell

A cat's sensitive nose can pick up scents over long distances. This helps big cats communicate with each other, find mates, and detect and track prey. Scents enter their nostrils and travel over smell receptors, where they can be identified.

The nose has no fur, making it highly sensitive to smells.

SOUND

Most big cats have large, movable ears to recognize sounds and the direction they are coming from. They can identify prey by the noises they make. Cats can detect some sounds that we humans cannot pick up.

TOUCH

Naturally cautious, big cats use their paws to feel and examine anything unfamiliar. Once they know it is safe, they use their nose and whiskers for further investigation.

Whiskers

Whiskers are an important tool that helps the other senses. These long, stiff hairs help big cats judge the nearness of prey in the dark. They also help with biting prey. Whiskers are pulled forward as cats bite, helping make the bite more accurate.

Whiskers have sensitive nerve endings at the roots.

Where cats live

Cats make their homes in many natural areas, called habitats. Each species has adapted to survive in its chosen habitat. These range from snowy mountains and swampy marshlands to scorching deserts and steamy rainforests.

Habitat loss

Today, many cats are under threat in their own habitats. A great number of forests have been cut down so that people can use the wood. Cutting down trees also makes space for farmland. This is called deforestation. As land is cleared, cats may lose their original territories and need to find new homes.

Deforestation of a forest

Desert

Life is tough for wild cats living in dry, barren deserts where water and food are limited. They must learn to survive for long periods of time without regular water.

Snowy mountains

The cold climates of mountain peaks and snowy forests suit some very big cats, including the Amur, or Siberian, tiger. Fur grows thicker and longer to keep them warm.

Grassland

The African grasslands are home to many big cats. Thick grass covers this habitat. However, there is not enough yearly rainfall for trees to grow.

Rainforest

Tropical rainforests are hot and very rainy. The thick green plants, flowing rivers, and mix of creatures help big cats survive and even thrive here.

Rocky mountains

Rocky mountains have high peaks, sharp drops, and tough ridges. Cats need to use their expert climbing and balancing skills to live in this landscape.

Wetlands

Some parts of the world can flood in heavy rain and soon become huge wetlands. Here, lots of animals make their homes in marshes and swamps.

Caracal
Caracal means "black ears." This cat uses its long legs to leap into the air and catch birds in the grasslands of Africa and the Middle East.

Snow leopard
This solitary cat roams some of the highest mountains in central Asia. It survives on a diet of goats, sheep, and hares.

Cheetah
This champion cat is faster than any other animal on earth. It has an athletic body and long legs, which help it hunt at breathtaking speed.

Bengal tiger
This big cat sits at the top of the food chain in the rainforests of Asia. Here, it has plenty of water to drink and lots of animals to eat.

Puma
The puma is also called a mountain lion. High up in the mountains of the Americas, it uses its powerful back legs and large claws to scramble across difficult ground.

Jaguar
This cool cat is at home in the wetlands of Central and South America. It patrols the riverbanks, hunting prey on land or in water.

Water dwellers

Although most domestic cats hate water, some wild ones are happy to make a splash! Several species are skilled swimmers. They will enter rivers and lakes to catch prey, cool off, or simply enjoy a bath.

! WOW

While **all cats can swim**, few of them choose to, and most prefer to **stay on dry land.**

FACT FILE

» **Regions:** South and Central America

» **Location:** Amazon basin

Jaguar

The jaguar enjoys regular swims in the American tropics. Here, the many rivers and streams are a perfect hunting ground for prey ranging in size from fish to crocodiles.

Caimans are among the preferred prey of jaguars in water.

White-tailed deer can swim across rivers and are a target for tigers.

Swimming lessons

Some cats coax their cubs into the water to help them get used to it. Cubs learn to swim by watching their mother and following what she does.

Mountain lion cub swimming

Fishing cat

This wild cat lives in the wetlands of Asia. The fishing cat is suited to living and hunting in water. It has webbed toes on its front paws.

FACT FILE

» **Regions:** India and Indonesia

» **Location:** mangrove forests of the Sundarbans

Fishing cats dive underwater and grasp fish with their sharp claws.

Tigers

The biggest of the big cats is also among the strongest swimmers. However, tigers are more likely to use rivers to cool down than to hunt.

FACT FILE

» **Regions:** Asia

» **Location:** India, Siberia, and parts of Southeast Asia

Snow leopards

One of the world's rarest big cats lives a lonely existence on the snowy slopes of central Asia. Blending in with the mountains, the nimble-footed snow leopard is able to leap and chase prey downhill. It uses its amazing strength to catch and bring down goats, sheep, and other prey.

Thick fur
Long, thick, woolly fur is necessary to keep the snow leopard warm in freezing temperatures.

Long tail
The huge, furry tail is almost half the entire length of the snow leopard. It helps with balance on rocky ground and offers a warm blanket to snuggle with in the snow.

The mysterious cat

The secretive snow leopard is difficult to spot because of its color and location. Because of this, it's difficult to say how many there are. Footprints in the snow, traces of pee (urine), and scratch marks on trees all give clues about numbers.

Footprints of a snow leopard

Short ears

The ears are shorter and smaller than those of most big cats, which helps reduce heat loss in the icy environment.

Nasal cavity

As the snow leopard breathes in the chilly air, its large nasal cavity (hollow space) warms up the breath on its way to the lungs.

Strong muscles

Lined with muscles, the powerful chest gives the snow leopard the strength to climb across rocks easily.

Padded paws

All four puffy paws are cushioned to keep the heat inside and stop the snow leopard from sinking into deep snow.

Spot the difference!

Leopards and cheetahs are often mistaken for each other, but there are big differences between them. Cheetahs live mainly on grasslands and chase their prey. Leopards can live in many habitats, including grasslands. They stalk their prey before pouncing.

A leopard's head is larger than a cheetah's.

Leopard

Leopards live in Africa and parts of Asia. Leopards are short and stocky. They are stronger and more muscular than cheetahs.

Leopards have rosettes. These help them hide in dense foliage (plants).

The leopard's tail helps it balance while climbing trees.

Leopards have retractable claws. This means they can be withdrawn or extended.

Grass is greener

In addition to the mighty lion, there are other, smaller wild cats that live in the grasslands. These cats are harder to spot, but their lifestyle is similar to that of big cats.

A Pallas's cat walking in the wild

Pallas's cat
This small wild cat lives in grasslands high up in central Asia. It is named after the German naturalist Peter Simon Pallas, who described this species in 1776.

Cheetah

Like leopards, cheetahs live mainly on the African grasslands. They are also found in parts of western Asia. They are tall, thin cats that are incredibly fast, with less heavy muscle than a leopard.

Cheetahs have tear marks on their faces.

A cheetah's tail is flat and helps it steer while running.

Cheetahs have a spotted coat that helps them hide in open grasslands. This is called camouflage.

Cheetahs have semi-retractable claws, which help them grip the ground while running, in the same way running spikes help a sprinter.

A jungle cat peering through grass

Jungle cat
Despite its name, the jungle cat lives in grasslands and swamps. Its large ears can detect even the quietest prey moving in thick vegetation.

An African wildcat in the desert

African wildcat
Looking like a large domestic cat, the African wildcat hunts in open grassland and desert. This skilled climber hides from predators in trees.

Climbing cats

Trees provide a safe place for many cats. High branches offer cats the best view of their surroundings and a great place to catnap. Cats can also hide behind dense leaves. This helps them avoid predators, stalk prey, and feast on dead animals, away from hungry scavengers.

Leopard

This expert climber is the biggest cat to climb trees. Leopards carry their prey into the treetops to avoid packs of hyenas or jackals moving in to steal their food.

Top cats

Smaller cats use their light frames and sharp claws to climb trees easily. High branches offer a clear view of the grasslands and forests below.

A margay prepares to leap.

Margay
Margays are small wild cats with long legs and long tails, who leap through the trees of South America. In the forest treetops, they can find plenty of birds and squirrels to eat.

A clouded leopard views the forest below.

Clouded leopard
This nimble-footed cat prowls high up in the trees of the dense forests of Southeast Asia. The clouded leopard is a secretive animal that is hard to spot. It is one of the best climbers of all cats. It can rotate (turn) its back paws and run headfirst down a tree, like a squirrel!

! WOW!

Leopards can **carry prey** weighing nearly **twice** their own body weight!

Movement

Meet the world's fastest animal on land. This incredible cat can travel as fast as a car on the highway while hunting prey in the African grasslands.

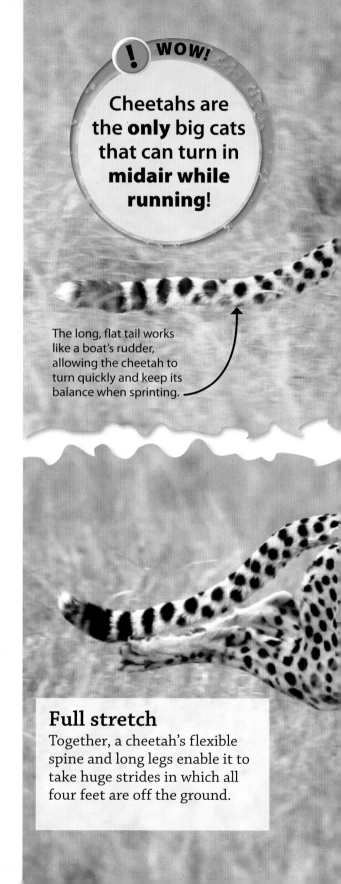

The long, flat tail works like a boat's rudder, allowing the cheetah to turn quickly and keep its balance when sprinting.

Safe landing

The saying goes that cats have nine lives. Although this is not true, cats are great at jumping and landing safely. Cats have a built-in righting reflex that helps them twist around in midair and land on their feet.

During a fall, the cat first levels its head, ready to turn.

The cat rotates its chest and front legs to turn itself right-side up.

The back legs turn and straighten out in preparation to hit the ground.

Now fully flipped over, the cat lands on its feet, which absorb the shock.

Full stretch

Together, a cheetah's flexible spine and long legs enable it to take huge strides in which all four feet are off the ground.

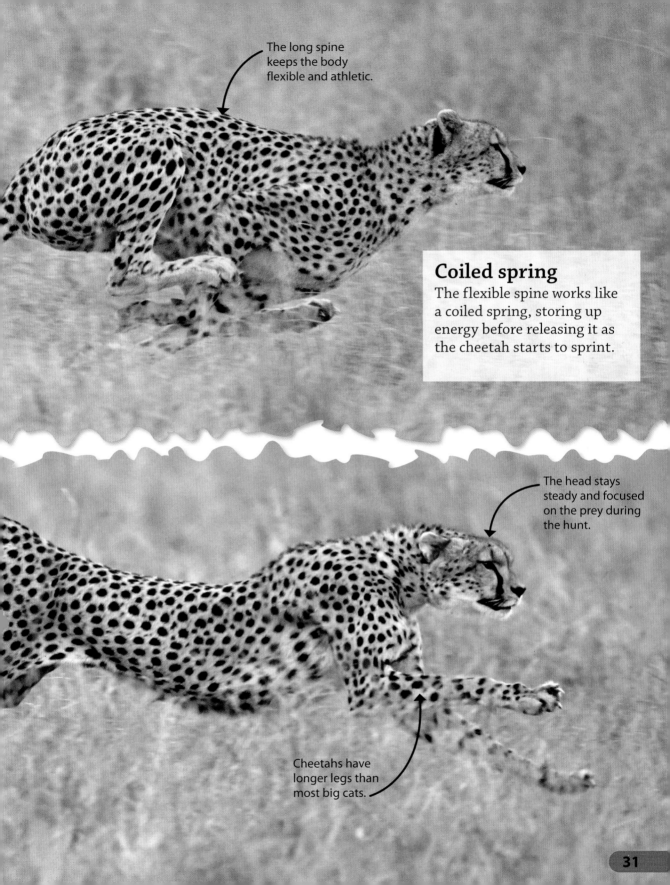

The long spine keeps the body flexible and athletic.

Coiled spring
The flexible spine works like a coiled spring, storing up energy before releasing it as the cheetah starts to sprint.

The head stays steady and focused on the prey during the hunt.

Cheetahs have longer legs than most big cats.

Pride of lions

Sociable lions are the only big cats to live in groups, called prides. Each family member has its own role to fulfill. Lions communicate by roaring, growling, and licking each other. Prides live freely on African grasslands, with no natural predators but plenty of prey to target and eat.

Lion

A male lion's job is to defend the pride's territory. There are only one or two males in most prides. They roar loudly and use scent markings to warn other males to stay away.

Lioness

Females outnumber the males in every pride. Hardworking lionesses do most of the hunting and care for their young. Every two years, a lioness gives birth to a litter of up to five cubs.

Cubs

The average pride has about 12 cubs. They learn to hunt by watching the lionesses in action. Cubs play fight and chase each other, helping them grow in strength and confidence.

Mane attraction

The majestic mane of the lion shows its power and position in the pride. A thick mane also makes the lion appear larger to other males. Lionesses do not have manes because this would weigh them down when hunting.

Lioness and lion

On a hunt

As darkness falls on the African savannah, lionesses gather in groups to plan the night's work. With meat on their minds, they must work as a team to ensure the pride does not go hungry.

The adult lionesses wait until night falls to start their organized operation. This time of day is much cooler, so they use less energy.

After spotting prey, by sight or sound, lionesses lie low. Then they start to move toward their target, slowly and silently...

The younger lionesses begin the chase first because they are the quickest and strongest. This teamwork is a strength of lions, who are not the fastest of the big cats. The prey—a large group of zebras—runs away, fast...

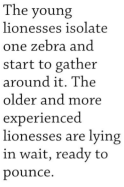

The young lionesses isolate one zebra and start to gather around it. The older and more experienced lionesses are lying in wait, ready to pounce.

The lionesses attack! They bring the zebra to the ground. They bite into the zebra's flesh. The lone zebra has no chance against so many lions. Even very large prey are a potential kill when outnumbered by attackers.

Now the feeding hierarchy gets underway. If the lion is present, he must feast first. The cubs join him later, before the lionesses get the leftovers. A large kill satisfies the pride for a week before another hunt begins.

Night prowlers

Most cats don't waste time sleeping at night! Many are up and about, using the darkness to their advantage. During these action-packed hours, cats hunt and feed. Animals that are awake at night and sleep during the day are called nocturnal. Nocturnal activities are possible because big cats can see just as well at night as they do during the day, but unsuspecting prey cannot see them.

! WOW!

A big cat on the **hunt** was recorded traveling more than **25 miles (40 km) in one night!**

Hunting at night

Midnight feast
After a successful hunt, this leopard has dragged its prey up into a tree to eat. Being high up keeps the food away from other animals that may smell the dead animal and move in.

Bright eyes
Like all wild cats, the eyes of this sand cat appear to glow in the dark. A special reflective layer helps the eyes absorb as much light as possible.

Light-reflecting eyes

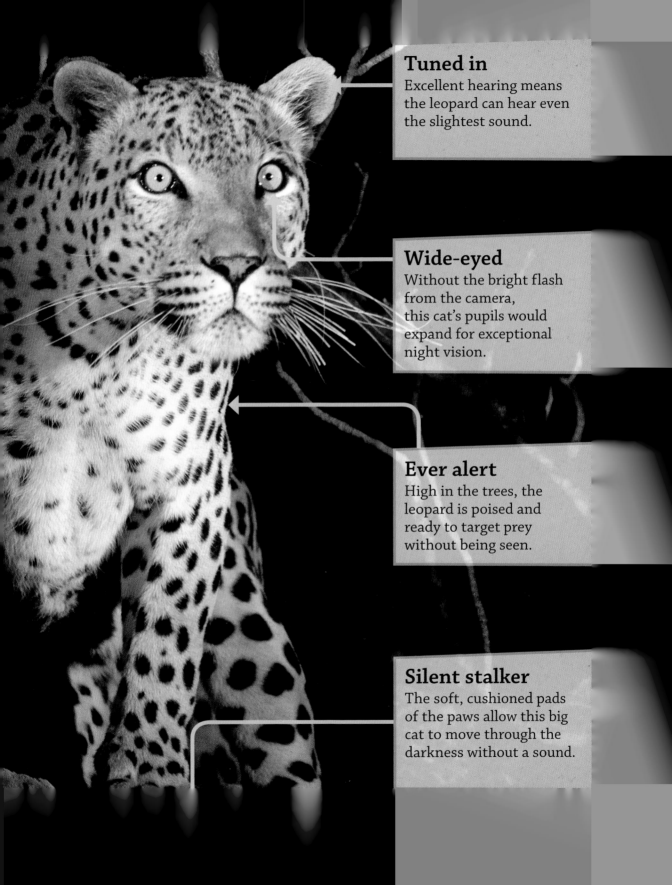

Tuned in
Excellent hearing means the leopard can hear even the slightest sound.

Wide-eyed
Without the bright flash from the camera, this cat's pupils would expand for exceptional night vision.

Ever alert
High in the trees, the leopard is poised and ready to target prey without being seen.

Silent stalker
The soft, cushioned pads of the paws allow this big cat to move through the darkness without a sound.

Cat sounds

Big cats and other wild cats communicate in a variety of ways and always make themselves heard. From grunting and growling to hissing and snarling, these sounds can be signs of aggression or happiness, or simple forms of communication with other cats or wild animals.

Growl

Watch out! Tigers and other big cats often growl as the first sign of aggression. This warns other animals that an attack is likely unless they leave or retreat.

Chirp

Among the softest speakers of the cat world, cheetahs cannot roar. Instead they produce a distinctive chirping sound to show affection or attract a mate.

Purr

Pumas purr just as domestic cats and kittens do. Purring is a sign of satisfaction or affection. It can also be the sound of a mother bonding with her cubs.

Snarl

Jaguars and many wild cats snarl in a clear display of fear or anger. They might also flatten their ears and bare their sharp teeth to make sure their feelings are understood.

Hiss

This serval is sending out a warning to rivals or predators. Hissing suggests a cat feels threatened and will fight if necessary.

Roar

Lions are the loudest cats. A booming roar from a lion is often a warning to a rival to stay away from the lion and his pride. Lionesses roar, but their roar is softer than the male's. While the main big cats roar, smaller wild cats and domestic cats cannot.

REALLY?

!

A lion's roar can be heard **5 miles (8 km) away!**

Tigers

The tiger is the world's largest and heaviest big cat. There are five types (called subspecies) of tiger, and they all live in Asia. Whether living in tropical rainforest or snow-covered woodland, they all depend on forest habitats, which provide water and food for survival.

Tigers are from Asia, the largest continent in the world.

India

A group of Bengal tigers

Bengal tiger
Bengal tigers live mostly in India. There are more Bengal tigers than any other type of tiger. Some live in mangrove forest swamps called the Sundarbans. However, the destruction of forests and illegal hunting mean there are now fewer Bengal tigers than ever before.

Indochinese tiger
At home in Southeast Asia, the Indochinese tiger uses its powerful legs to run and swim after prey. Its striped coat gives it great camouflage—helping it hide behind trees before pouncing.

An Indochinese tiger

Amur tiger

The Amur tiger, also known as the Siberian tiger, is the largest of the big cats and lives in the coldest climate. Having the longest, thickest fur coat helps this tiger stay warm during snowy Siberian winters.

A Siberian tiger in the Sikhote-Alin mountain range

Russia

Vietnam

Malaysia

Indonesia

A Malayan tiger in wetland habitat

Malayan tiger

This small tiger roams the forests of south Thailand and west Malaysia. It hunts deer, boar, and goats in leafy forests and enjoys swimming in wetlands.

Sumatran tiger

The Sumatran tiger lives on the Indonesian island of Sumatra. The smallest tiger in the world, this big cat is 30 percent smaller and weighs 50 percent less than the biggest big cat, the Siberian tiger.

A Sumatran tiger resting

Catnaps

Big cats spend much of their time asleep. This isn't because they are lazy, but because they don't want to waste energy. They prefer lots of short power naps to one long sleep. In hot countries, the daylight hours of scorching sunshine are best for sleeping, leaving dawn, dusk, and nighttime for hunting.

Sleep sites

Wild cats must consider the best place to sleep. Cool places offer protection from the heat, while sheltered spots are perfect hideouts from rivals or predators.

A lazy leopard napping on a tree branch

Shady snooze
Trees offer a welcome retreat for tired leopards. Here they can nap high in the branches, away from prying eyes.

Lounging lions

Lion prides like to sleep in the shade of trees. Lions are at the top of the food chain, so they have no predators.

Solitary sleep
Any lion without an established pride is vulnerable. They must stay awake longer or rest with one eye open to watch for signs of danger.

! WOW!

Big cats in the wild can **sleep** or **rest** for more than **18 hours** a day!

A lion rests with one eye open to look out for danger

Marking territories

Many cats create their own areas, called territories, and adopt different ways to mark them. Territories vary in size but need to contain enough prey for the cats to hunt. Boundaries are marked to warn other cats to stay away, but if a rival strays into another territory, fights can result.

Scratching
Like most big cats, lions love scratching tree trunks. This cleans and sharpens their claws and keeps them in good condition. It also marks their territory with a scent, so other cats can tell where they have been.

Vocalizing
From this hissing serval to the roaring lion, wild cats use aggressive noises to scare enemies away. Spitting and gritting teeth are two other ways that cats keep territories clear of rivals.

Cub care

Male big cats may attack and kill the cubs of rival males in the fight to win a mate. Females try to protect their young by taking them away from the danger zone and creating a safe den in which to raise them. They carry cubs gently by the nape (back) of their necks and hide them in thick foliage (plants) for safety.

A female leopard carrying her cub

Scenting

This cheetah is marking its territory with scent marks to warn that the area is already taken. Its scent is mixed with urine (pee). It is sprayed along territory lines and on trees to stop rivals from crossing territory borders. The scent can last for weeks.

Fighting over turf

Tigers are one of many types of big cat that will fight to keep control of a territory. Competition for the same mate can also cause aggressive fights between cats.

Playtime

It can't be all work and no play for big cats! In the time between hunting, sleeping, and eating, they entertain themselves and form friendships. Cubs in particular love to play. They grow in confidence by copying adult behavior and learn essential survival techniques, too.

Tree climbing
Cubs learn how to climb trees by following their mothers. Tree climbing is just for fun while cats are young, but it becomes an important survival skill in later life.

Play fighting
Young cubs enjoy play fighting together, which helps build physical strength, encourages self-defense, and teaches hunting techniques.

Tail play
Playful cubs practice their hunting skills by trying to catch their mother's tail. This speeds up their reactions in preparation for chasing live prey.

Rolling

A happy big cat rolls around on its back, enjoying the freedom and relaxation. By revealing his tummy, this lion shows he feels secure in his pride.

Swimming

Tigers are strong swimmers and will often take dips to cool off or just for their own enjoyment.

Rubbing

Big cats show affection by rubbing and licking each other's heads. This process exchanges individual scents and strengthens social bonds.

Grooming

Big cats see grooming as a sociable activity and take time to clean each other's fur. This helps them identify one another by their scent. Mothers keep their cubs clean using their rough tongues to remove dirt and tangles.

Meet the expert

Giles Clark is the director of big cats and conservation at the Big Cat Sanctuary in Kent, England. The sanctuary houses more than 50 cats and supports conservation projects overseas.

Q: We know it has something to do with cats, but what is your actual job?

A: Firstly, I help my team look after our cats here at the Big Cat Sanctuary. This means making sure we take care of all their needs and keep them active. Secondly, I help oversee education programs—spreading awareness about endangered animals is an important part of my job. Finally, I help decide how we can assist conservation projects and programs working to save wild cats and their natural habitats.

Q: What made you want to work with cats?

A: Some of my earliest and fondest memories growing up as a young boy are of the many domestic cats my parents used to take in and rescue. Some of these cats were my first friends, and it was being around them that allowed me to develop a passion and respect for all cats—big and small!

Q: What is it about big cats that you love?

A: I find all cats fascinating. There are 40 species of cats that have spanned almost the entire planet, all with similar characteristics and traits, and yet each species is unique and perfectly adapted to its own environment at the same time. Domestic cats are the most popular pet in the world, and if you watch how they live in your house and garden, you will see many behaviors they have that are very similar to their wild cousins'.

Q: Why are big cats important?

Cats are such a vital part of the ecosystems where they live. Big cats are at the top of the food chain and help maintain a healthy balance in nature. To save these magnificent

Giles with a Sumatran tiger and cub at Australia Zoo, Queensland, Australia

species, we must protect their habitats. In turn, this will save all the other species that live in the same habitats, from the smallest of insects to primates in the trees. Cats kept in zoos and sanctuaries help scientists learn and understand more about these species. This knowledge can be used to help cats in the wild and help awareness of conservation issues.

Q: Do you have a favorite species of cat?

A: It's almost impossible for me to choose a favorite species of cat! I have spent many years looking after tigers so will always have a special place for them in my heart. Equally, the clouded leopard is another species that I find absolutely incredible.

Q: Do you have any cats of your own?

A: I have always had cats at home and sometimes not always domestic cats! Over the years, I have been required to hand raise several cubs that have needed special care and attention, most recently a baby jaguar called Maya who was only six days old when

Giles with Maya the jaguar

she arrived. Like her mom would have, I fed her through the night for the first few months. I did this until she was about three months old and strong enough to live back at the sanctuary. Wild animals don't make good pets though—they can be dangerous when they start to grow up.

Q: What is the most difficult part of your job?

A: Saying goodbye to some of the cats I have cared for is always very difficult. The other thing I find very hard is knowing that so many species of cats are endangered and risk becoming extinct in the wild because of humans and our actions.

Q: What is the best thing about your job?

A: The best part of my job is knowing that I get to make a difference, not only improving the lives of the cats I help look after but also helping protect them in the wild. I always get excited talking to people about how important it is to protect our natural world and all the amazing species we share the planet with. For a long time, humans have been part of the problem for cats in the wild, but now we can be part of the solution!

Playing with a serval

Under threat

Today, the number of cats in the wild has fallen dramatically to very low levels. People are ultimately to blame, from hunting wild cats to destroying their homes. The growing world population has affected the environment and changed natural habitats forever, causing wild cats and their prey to face an ongoing struggle for survival.

Deforestation

Big cats, including tigers and jaguars, have seen their habitats disappear when people cut down trees and clear the land. Large areas of forest have been destroyed.

Deforestation in the Amazon rainforest, Brazil

Further farmland

Many areas of forest and grassland have been turned into farmland, leaving less space for wild cats. Because jaguars and cheetahs have attacked farm animals, farmers set traps to stop them.

Illegal trade

Sadly, in some countries today, the illegal buying and selling of animal fur and bones is still taking place. Tigers and cheetahs are among the victims of these illegal hunters.

High-profile campaigns have highlighted the cruelty of wearing animal fur.

Snow leopards are forced to move higher up the mountains as people move in.

Population explosion

With the world population increasing, there is less room for wild cats than before. Their habitats shrink to make room for more housing for humans.

Trophy hunting

Hunters consider lions the top prize. Although laws have been introduced to protect wild cats, illegal hunting continues.

Limited prey

Wild cats are facing a reduced food supply. They must compete with other animals for the same prey. People also hunt the prey of wild cats, leaving them with even less food.

Animals such as antelopes are a target for many meat eaters (carnivores).

Endangered or extinct?

When a big cat species declines in number, it is given a rank to describe how threatened it is and how likely the species is to become extinct in the future. Threatened species are given the rank of vulnerable, endangered, or critically endangered, according to how high the threat level is. If a species dies out completely, it is called extinct.

The American lion became extinct 11,000 years ago.

How we're helping

Today, there are many ways we can help protect big cats and aid their survival. Conservation efforts are underway around the world to help boost the numbers of big cats. Some big cats live in protected areas, and new laws are being introduced to stop hunting.

Trained staff work closely alongside the big cats.

A keeper training a cheetah

Sanctuaries

Keeping big cats in animal sanctuaries means that they have a regular food supply, are safe from human hunters, and enjoy a longer life expectancy. Sanctuaries and safari parks also use breeding programs to increase big cats' numbers, with some cats being released back into the wild.

The Big Cat Sanctuary in Kent, England, holds more than 50 cats.

REALLY?

In **2016,** tiger numbers **increased** for the first time in a century.

Anti-poaching laws

The introduction of new laws to ban hunting and poaching has helped protect the world's big cats. Further measures have been taken to enforce the bans and deter illegal hunting.

Educating

Teaching children about big cats and conservation in local schools is an important way of encouraging future generations to play their part in protecting the planet's wildlife.

A conservationist teaching a class in South Africa

Lessons on conservation show children how to live alongside and help wildlife.

Tracking cats

Keeping track of big cats helps conservationists understand the threats facing them. A Global Positioning System (GPS) collar reveals a big cat's movements and what they do.

A GPS collar helps track a cat's movements and is completely harmless.

Conservation projects

Many conservation projects focus on replanting trees to rebuild natural habitats and encourage big cats to return.

Anti-poaching dogs protect Kenya's endangered wildlife.

A community in the Amazon rainforest planting tree seedlings

BASTET

In ancient Egypt, cats were worshipped as gods, and any ill-treatment of one could be punishable by death. Bastet was an Egyptian goddess whose symbol was the cat. The goddess was believed to protect those who worshipped her.

JAGUARS

The jaguar featured in Aztec and Maya cultures in Mexico and Central America. Aztec warriors dressed as jaguars because they believed it would give them strength and provide protection when fighting a war.

Legends

Throughout history, cats have played an important part in the cultures and religions of many countries around the world. In some societies, such as ancient Egypt, cats have been worshipped as gods. It's been said that cats have a mysterious, aloof quality, or aura. Perhaps it's this that has captured the hearts and minds of people for centuries and which continues to do so today.

DAWON

In Hindu religious mythology in India, Dawon was a terrifying tiger who symbolized power. The goddess Durga would ride Dawon into battle. While Durga fought with weapons, Dawon used its claws and teeth.

HAECHI

The lion has long been seen as a protector in Asia. This big cat featured in Indian and Chinese art before reaching Korea. Here it was named Haechi and carved into wood and stone sculptures.

Good fortune

Cats are considered lucky in many places. The maneki-neko, or "beckoning cat," remains a lucky talisman in Japan. A raised right paw means good luck, while a raised left one means welcome. The Buddhist faith, based on the teachings of the Buddha, also holds cats in high esteem. Buddhists believe that when a person dies, their soul goes to a cat for safekeeping.

Maneki-neko

The Buddha with three big cats

Ancient ancestors

The first wild cats stalked this planet many millions of years ago. The discovery of fossils has helped us understand ancient cats. Fossils show us that in many ways, ancient cats were similar to modern big cats, but that over time, big cats have developed sharp teeth and claws, two important features that they can't live without today.

» Scale

Miacis

A fossil discovered in Germany revealed a cat that looked like a long-legged weasel. Miacis lived about 56–34 million years ago. It was an excellent climber that used its long tail for balancing on tree branches.

» Scale

Xenosmilus

This powerful cat lived in North America around one million years ago. Its heavy weight made chasing prey difficult. Instead, Xenosmilus used trees for cover before pouncing on passing prey, including wild pigs.

Dinictis

The same size as a serval, Dinictis prowled the grasslands of North America looking for prey around 34–20 million years ago. While today most cats walk on their toes, a fossil found in South Dakota proved this ancient cat was very flat-footed.

» Scale

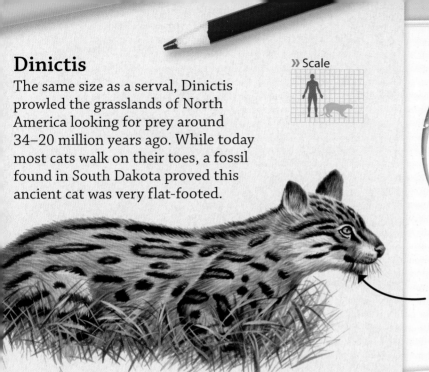

! WOW!

The **oldest fossils** relating to the **cat family** are **50 million years old!**

Beneath its soft fur and small skull, Dinictis hid dagger-like canine teeth.

Smilodon

Snarling Smilodon is known for its massive fangs. Saber-toothed (meaning "sword-toothed") cats used their terrific teeth to stab huge prey, including mammoth and bison. Like modern-day lions, sociable Smilodon lived and hunted in groups, before becoming extinct about 12,000 years ago.

» Scale

Smilodon teeth could reach 20 in (50 cm) in length and never stopped growing!

Big cat facts and figures

Big cats are among the fastest and strongest animals and some of the most successful carnivores on earth. Read on for some cat facts to really sink your teeth into...

Of all the cats, **servals** have the **biggest ears** and **legs** compared to the rest of their **body**.

No big cat species is **indigenous** to (originates in) the continent of **Australia**.

A cheetah can reach **70 mph (112 kph)** in just **3 seconds**.

4 IN

A lion's canine tooth, including the root, is 4 in (10 cm) long. An adult human's canine is only ½ in (1.5 cm) long.

50%

About half of all species of wild cat are vulnerable, endangered, or critically endangered.

The word *jaguar* is derived from the Native American word *yaguar*, which means "**he who kills with one leap**."

The male lions of **TSAVO** in Kenya **have short and tufted manes**, like a bad haircut!

A **jaguar's jaws** are strong enough to crack open tortoise shells—helping it get to one of its favorite treats.

550 LB

The average male Siberian tiger weighs 550 lb (250 kg)—that's equal to more than 60 domestic cats!

2,500

The approximate number of spots on an adult cheetah.

Glossary

Here are the meanings of some words that are useful for you to know when learning all about big cats.

accelerate Speed up

ambush Unexpected attack from a hidden position

apex predator Predator at the top of the food chain

aquatic Living in water

camouflage Colors or patterns on an animal's skin or fur that help it blend in with its surroundings

canine Large, pointed tooth belonging to a mammal

captivity State of being confined or enclosed and prevented from escaping

carnivore Animal that eats meat

conservation Saving the environment, which includes attempts to protect endangered animals and stop them from becoming extinct

cranium Area of the skull protecting the brain

cub The young of wild animals, such as lions, cheetahs, or tigers

deforestation The cutting down of a forest or large expanse of trees

domesticated Animals kept as pets or living on farms

ecosystem Plants and animals that live in an area and the relationship that exists between them and their habitat

endangered Species low in numbers that could become extinct

environment Surroundings in which an animal lives

extinct When a species dies out so none are left in the world

feline Member of the cat family

feral Animal living in the wild that was once domesticated or in captivity

food chain Series of living things in which each thing feeds on the next one

fossil Remains of a dead animal that has become embedded in rock and preserved over time

A puma is a large and powerful carnivore.

habitat Natural home environment of an animal

indigenous Originating or occurring naturally in a particular place

instinct An animal's natural response to a situation

kill Animal or animals killed during a hunt

lineage Generations of the same family

mammal Warm-blooded, vertebrate animals that have skin covered in hair. Females feed their young milk

migration Movement of people or animals from one place to another

naturalist Expert in the scientific study of animals or plants

nocturnal Animal that is active at night to hunt or feed

poaching Illegal hunting of wild animals

predator Animal that naturally hunts other living animals for food

prey Animal that is hunted and killed for food

pride Family group of lions

rainforest Thick forest of tall trees and other vegetation that is found in tropical areas

reproduce To have young

retractable Something that can be drawn back, for example, claws

rival Animal competing for the same territory or mate

sanctuary Safe haven from danger

savannah Area of grassland with few trees

scavenger Animal that feeds on the remains of another animal that is already dead

scent Individual smell produced by an animal

senses Sight, smell, hearing, taste, and touch are senses

sociable Friendly interaction with other members of the same species

solitary Animal that lives alone

species A group of plants or animals that all share similar features or characteristics

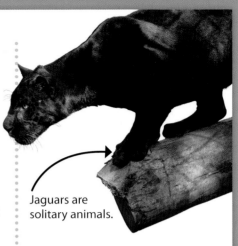

Jaguars are solitary animals.

subspecies A smaller group within a species that has specific features and a shared location

territory Area that is defended by an animal

tropical Area or climate with hot temperatures and high rainfall

vegetation Plant life found in a particular habitat

vertebrate Animal with a backbone

vulnerable Species likely to become endangered unless threats to its survival decrease

warm-blooded Animal that keeps a constant body temperature

Index

Acknowledgments

DORLING KINDERSLEY would like to thank the following: Polly Goodman for proofreading, Helen Peters for compiling the index, Richard Leeney for photography, and Dan Crisp for illustrations. The publishers would also like to thank Tanith Brown and the team at The Big Cat Sanctuary, and Giles Clark for the "Meet the Expert" interview and consultancy.

The publisher would like to thank the following for their kind permission to reproduce their photographs:

(Key: a-above; b-below/bottom; c-center; f-far; l-left; r-right; t-top)

1 **Dreamstime.com:** Isselee (c). 3 **Alamy Stock Photo:** VPC Animals Photo (bc). **Getty Images:** Anup Shah (bl). **The Big Cat Sanctuary, UK:** (crb). 4 **123RF.com:** Anan Kaewkhammul / anankkml (ca, c). **The Big Cat Sanctuary, UK:** (cra). 4-5 **Dorling Kindersley:** Wildlife Heritage Foundation, Kent, UK (c). 5 **Dreamstime.com:** Isselee (cr). 6 **123RF.com:** Thorsten Nilson. 7 **123RF.com:** Ana Vasileva / ABV. 8 **Dreamstime.com:** Isselee (bl). 9 **123RF.com:** Anan Kaewkhammul / anankkml (cl); Anan Kaewkhammul (t). **Dorling Kindersley:** Wildlife Heritage Foundation, Kent, UK (bl). 10 **Alamy Stock Photo:** Julie Mowbray. 11 **The Big Cat Sanctuary, UK:** (tr). 13 **Alamy Stock Photo:** VPC Animals Photo (c). **Dreamstime.com:** Eastmanphoto (t). 14 **Dorling Kindersley:** Wildlife Heritage Foundation, Kent, UK (cla). **Fotolia:** Kevin Moore (cl). 15 **Alamy Stock Photo:** Redmond Durrell (cra, cr). **Dorling Kindersley:** Wildlife Heritage Foundation, Kent, UK (cla, cl). 16 **iStockphoto.com:** Freder (br). 17 **Dreamstime.com:** Outdoorsman (bc). 18 **Dorling Kindersley:** Wildlife Heritage Foundation, Kent, UK (t, br). 21 **Ardea:** M. Watson (ca). **Depositphotos Inc:** Nicunickie1 (cb). **FLPA:** Chris Brunskill (bc); Sebastian Kennerknecht / Minden Pictures (cb/Mountain Lion). **iStockphoto.com:** Ajlber (t). **naturepl. com:** Peter Blackwell (ca/Cheetah resting). 22 **123RF.com:** Johnny Lye (cl). **Dreamstime. com:** Mikael Males (bc). 22-23 **Dreamstime. com:** Tony Northrup / Acanonguy (bc). 23 **123RF.com:** Ondrej Prosicky (b). **Alamy Stock Photo:** Arco Images GmbH (tr). 24-25 **Getty Images:** Don Johnston. 25 **iStockphoto.com:** Koonyongyut (tr). 26 **iStockphoto.com:** GlobalP (c). **naturepl.com:** Staffan Widstrand (br). 27 **123RF.com:** Nico Smit (br). **Alamy**

Stock Photo: Beata Aldridge (bl). **iStockphoto.com:** GlobalP (c). 28-29 **Rex by Shutterstock:** imageBROKER. 29 **Alamy Stock Photo:** Bill Attwell (crb). **iStockphoto. com:** KeithSzafranski (cra). 30 **Alamy Stock Photo:** Juniors Bildarchiv GmbH (l). 30-31 **naturepl.com:** Andy Rouse (t, b). 32-33 **FLPA:** Edward Myles. 36 **Alamy Stock Photo:** AfriPics.com (cl); Malcolm Schuyl (bc). 36-37 **Alamy Stock Photo:** David Cantrille. 38 **123RF.com:** Wavebreak Media Ltd (bl). 39 **Alamy Stock Photo:** Amazon-Images (tr); Life on white (br). **Dreamstime.com:** Richie Lomba (tl). 40 **iStockphoto.com:** Guenterguni (clb); David O'Brien (br). 40-41 **Dreamstime. com:** Piotr Adamowicz / Simpson333 (Background). 41 **Dreamstime.com:** Seread (tc); Sharkphoto (cr). 42-43 **naturepl.com:** Anup Shah. 42 **Alamy Stock Photo:** Jez Bennett (bc). 43 **Alamy Stock Photo:** Graham Prentice (bl). 44 **Getty Images:** Hoberman Collection / UIG (r); hphimagelibrary (l). 45 **123RF.com:** Simon Eeman (tr). **Getty Images:** Anup Shah (br). **iStockphoto.com:** Richmatts (l). 46 **123RF.com:** Andrey Gudkov (cla). **Alamy Stock Photo:** Avalon / Photoshot License (c); André Gilden (b). 47 **Alamy Stock Photo:** Safari_Pics (t). **Dreamstime.com:** Appfind (cl); Villiers Steyn (b). **iStockphoto. com:** RolfSt (cr). 48 **Giles Clark:** (bl). **The Big Cat Sanctuary, UK:** (tr). 49 **The Big Cat Sanctuary, UK:** (tr, bl). 51 **Science Photo Library:** Mark Hallett Paleoart (br). 52-53 **Getty Images:** Liza van Devente / Foto24 / Gallo Images (b). 53 **Alamy Stock Photo:** imageBROKER (cr); Edward Parker (br). **FLPA:** Sebastian Kennerknecht / Minden Pictures (cla). 54 **Dreamstime.com:** Gator (tl); Piotr Pawinski (tr). 55 **Alamy Stock Photo:** Godong (br). **Dreamstime.com:** Zatletic (tl). 56 **Dreamstime.com:** Ccat82 (b/Background). **Science Photo Library:** Michael Long (cl). 57 **Dreamstime.com:** Ccat82 (t/Background, crb/ Background). **Science Photo Library:** DEAGOSTINI / UIG (cla); Spencer Sutton (crb/ Cat); Javier Trueba / MSF (bl). 58 **Dorling Kindersley:** Blackpool Zoo, Lancashire, UK

(br). **Dreamstime.com:** Tony Campbell (bl). 58-59 **Dreamstime.com:** Rgbe (c). 59 **Alamy Stock Photo:** Octavio Campos Salles (tl). Matt Berlin: (tr). **The Big Cat Sanctuary, UK:** (ftr). 62 **Dorling Kindersley:** Wildlife Heritage Foundation, Kent, UK (tl). 63 **Alamy Stock Photo:** Life on white (br)

Endpaper images: *Front:* **Ardea:** Nick Gordon cb; **Dreamstime.com:** Isselee fbr, Geoffrey Kuchera br, Lukas Blazek / Lukyslukys c, cb (Pallas's cat), Rafael Angel Irusta Machin / Broker cb (Lynx); **The Big Cat Sanctuary, UK:** cb (Puma), bc; *Back:* **Dorling Kindersley:** Wildlife Heritage Foundation, Kent, UK tc, crb; **Dreamstime.com:** Geoffrey Kuchera tl; **The Big Cat Sanctuary, UK:** cl, bl, cra, bc

Cover images: *Front:* **Dreamstime.com:** Hel080808 cra, Isselee l, cb, br, Boleslaw Kubica cr; *Back:* **123RF.com:** Ana Vasileva / ABV cr; **Dorling Kindersley:** Wildlife Heritage Foundation, Kent, UK bl; *Front Flap:* **Alamy Stock Photo:** Avalon / Photoshot License br, Life on white cr, Julie Mowbray cl; **Dreamstime.com:** Gator bl/ (2); **Fotolia:** Kevin Moore clb; **Getty Images:** Don Johnston cra; **Science Photo Library:** Javier Trueba / MSF bc; The Big Cat Sanctuary, UK: bl, cra/ (2); *Back Flap:* **Dorling Kindersley:** Natural History Museum, London cb/ (Gemstone), The University of Aberdeen tl; **NASA:** cb

All other images © Dorling Kindersley
For further information see:
www.dkimages.com

My Findout facts:

Cat continents

Bobcat
The most common wild cat in North America is the bobcat. It prefers dense vegetation and swampy wetlands.

Eurasian lynx
Across many parts of Europe and Asia, this wild cat blends in with its forest and woodland surroundings.

Puma
Located in North, Central, and South America, the puma is usually found on rocky mountains but also lives in tropical rainforests.

Black jaguar
The black version of a jaguar stalks the rainforests and swamps of South America by night.

Lion
Almost all wild lions live south of the Sahara desert in Africa, but small numbers live in the Gir Forest, in India.